WHO'S CALLING THE SHOTS?
Making Your Own Decisions
Dan Webster

9780891043855

Booklets available in this series by Dan Webster:

Can Anything Good Come Out of Losing?
  Coping with Loss (#93885)

Flirting with the Dark Side
  Evil and Its Influences (#93915)

When Faith Isn't Easy Anymore
  Second Thoughts on Staying Committed (#93907)

When You Feel Like Nobody Cares
  Dealing with Loneliness (#93869)

When Your Parents Call It Quits
  Surviving Family Breakdown (#93877)

Who's Calling the Shots?
  Making Your Own Decisions (#93850)

The Navigators is an international Christian organization. Jesus Christ gave His followers the Great Commission to go and make disciples (Matthew 28:19). The aim of The Navigators is to help fulfill that commission by multiplying laborers for Christ in every nation.

NavPress is the publishing ministry of The Navigators. NavPress publications are tools to help Christians grow. Although publications alone cannot make disciples or change lives, they can help believers learn biblical discipleship, and apply what they learn to their lives and ministries.

© 1991 by Dan Webster
All rights reserved. No part of this publication may be reproduced in any form without written permission from
  NavPress, P.O. Box 6000, Colorado Springs, CO 80934.
ISBN 08910-93850

Cover design: Ken Puckett Associates

Unless otherwise identified, all Scripture in this publication is paraphrased by the author. A version quoted is the *Holy Bible: New International Version* (NIV). Copyright © 1973, 1978, 1984, International Bible Society. Used by permission of Zondervan Bible Publishers.

Printed in the United States of America

FOR A FREE CATALOG OF
NAVPRESS BOOKS & BIBLE STUDIES,
CALL TOLL FREE 1-800-366-7788 (USA)
or 1-416-499-4615 (CANADA)

WHO'S CALLING THE SHOTS?
Making Your Own Decisions

The first time that I can remember allowing peer pressure to get me into trouble was when I was eleven years old—and on my way to becoming a criminal. It was my first major criminal act. The crime involved an Alpha-Beta Supermarket. My friend suggested, "Hey, we ought to hit the Alpha-Beta Market." At eleven years of age, going to "hit" the local supermarket meant stealing a bunch of candy, and then going home to eat it. Back then, I loved candy, and I'd do anything for it.

So, after we planned the caper, we made our "hit" on the Alpha-Beta. The plan involved wearing baggy sweaters so that we could jam all kinds of stuff down the sleeves and then walking out without being noticed. At that point in my life, I was extremely overweight, so adding candy to my sleeves wasn't very noticeable.

I stuffed massive amounts of candy

into my sweater sleeves, walked outside, and climbed on my Schwinn Stingray bike to ride home with my friend. However, the store manager intercepted us, stood right in front of my bike, and said to us, "Boys, do you have anything you didn't pay for?"

I didn't think it was possible for an eleven-year-old to experience cardiac arrest, but it was heart attack time. Oh, horrors! "No, uh, we don't have anything we didn't pay for!"

So he asked, "Well, what's that in your sleeve?"

"What sleeve?"

"The one on your arm!"

"What arm? Oh, you mean this! How did this get there?"

So, he came real close to me and took his big hand and squeezed right in that place beside your neck on the top of your shoulder, the place that drops you to your knees in a hurry. I know this, because I have three sons, and if they get out of control—boom, the big squeeze—and they're down. "Dad, I believe you . . . anything you want!"

Anyway, he walked us into the office and we unloaded all this stuff. Even I didn't realize how much we had ripped off. There was a mountain of candy just kind of sitting there on his desk.

"Is there anything else, boys?" There was a Snickers in my back pocket, so I laid it out on the table.

"Well, boys, how do you feel about this?"

"Oh, I don't feel too good about it."

And the guy said, "Listen, I'll tell you what. I'm not going to call your parents. I'm going to let you go home and tell your parents to call me."

I thought, *Oh, right, tell my dad face-to-face. Why don't you just shoot me right here?!* That would have been less traumatic and a lot less painful.

He said, "I think that it's important for you to tell your dads," and he took our names and phone numbers. You know, when you're eleven years old, you're just not hardened enough to lie in a convincing way, and besides, my mom shopped there all the time, so I knew I was in trouble.

I rode home on my bike, and my dad was home early (of course he just *had* to be early *that* day), and my father was the kind of father who didn't have to spank me to hurt me. He would just get one of those kinds of looks that would do it . . . . "My son? Doing that? Oh, it just tears my heart out!"

So, I said, "Dad, I've got some bad news for you."

"What's that?" he asked.

"You need to call the manager of the grocery store, the Alpha-Beta."

"Why do I have to do that?"

"Well, I got caught shoplifting candy."

And then came that look. Horrors! He put me in the car, and we drove there and he gave me a little speech. He said, "You *will* go up to the man, and you *will* look him in the eye, and you *will* apologize and volunteer to do whatever work around the store you have to do in order to make retribution for the candy you ripped off."

I walked back into the store with my father standing there at the door. I walked up to the manager and said, "Sir, I'm sorry. I'm eleven years old. I ripped you off. I'll pay you back. I'll do anything. Will you please forgive me for what I did wrong?"

He looked at me and said, "Son, I appreciate that. Yes, I'll forgive you, and you don't have to pay me back. But don't you ever do that again!"

"No problem!" I said.

Now, I got to thinking about that and wondered, *Why in the world would I do something like that?* Why would anyone rip off candy at eleven years of age except for stupidity, or poverty, or obesity? But the more I got to thinking about it, the more it seemed to boil down to two main reasons.

The first reason why we do stupid stuff—things that in our conscience and in our heart we know we shouldn't do—is *fear*. I was afraid that if I didn't go along with what my buddy Jimmy told me to do, I'd be left out. Rejected. I'd be considered a nerd. It's a terrifying thing to think about being left alone! It's a horrible thought to think that the whole crowd's going to do something, while you say, "Oh, I can't do that because I have a *conscience*!"

And your friends respond, "Oh, well, thank you very much! Goodbye!"

So, you stand there all alone with your clear conscience . . . but all alone. It creates tremendous fear. What do I do? Do I do what my conscience tells me to do and get left alone? Or do I go along with them and violate my conscience? I mean, fear can motivate people to do some rather crazy things.

You might have heard about a fire several years ago at a huge thoroughbred farm in Kentucky where they raised $250,000 to $500,000 thoroughbred horses. A barn was engulfed in flames, and the trainers were trying to get the beautiful, very costly horses out of the barn. They would take them to the door and hit them on the rump, and then the horses would go about three steps, turn around, and run right back into the fire. They couldn't get the horses to leave! They could lead them to the door, but because they were so terrified, they were completely irrational. They turned around and ran right back to their death.

Fear can also motivate us to do some rather crazy things. I didn't understand when I was eleven that Scripture says,

"Don't fear. The Lord is with you. What can a measly human being do to you?" (Psalm 118:6). At the age of eleven, I didn't understand that.

The second thing that drove me to the Alpha-Beta caper was *envy*. My logic was, "Hey, listen. I don't want to miss out on the fun." It's horrible to stand by and watch everybody partying, and you feel like you're kind of standing on the sidelines, while everybody else is out doing whatever they want, their consciences apparently not bothering them. Eventually you watch them partying, and you begin to envy them. You think, *Hey, you know, I want to be a part of this!* And to tell you the truth, at the age of eleven, I didn't want to be left out either. I wanted to be a part of the action.

A lot of us cave in under pressure, even when our consciences tell us that it's wrong. But because we envy many of the things that other people are doing, we're sort of pushed into doing them.

Fear and envy seem to be two major pressures that nudge us into doing the wrong things—fear of rejection and envy of missing out on something good in life. These peer pressures are intense for high school students today. But I also know that *it is possible* for students to desire spiritual growth so much that you choose to follow your conscience and devotion to God over the pressure and whims of the world around you. Many teens have this kind of desire, but lack the practical understanding of what to do in the pressure of the moment. Since we're not prepared for the pressure of those moments when people say, "C'mon, do this!" we cave in. Why? Either we fear rejection or we have an "I don't want to miss this!" attitude, so we jump right into it.

Here are three thoughts you could hold on to to help you through those moments of pressure, to help you resist doing the things that you know are wrong.

You need to allow God to tell you who you are, rather than allowing people to tell you who you are. We all tend to see ourselves through the eyes of the most important people in our lives. In other words, we allow them to tell us who we are.

If you live in a relationship with God, you allow *Him* to tell you who you are. And who you then perceive yourself to be will determine the choices you make in life. Who you walk most closely with is going to determine who you become.

I had a friend in ninth grade who was riding on the back of a motorcycle in Iowa. The cycle had a blowout, and she went flying through the air about thirty feet and came down. Her leg snapped. The doctors had to amputate her leg right above the knee because the knee joint was all messed up. She walked through life handicapped, partially crippled. In high school, she struggled with a lot of peer pressure.

When she graduated from high school, for her graduation present, her family took her on a cruise to Alaska. While on this cruise ship, she had to walk by all the beautiful young women tanning themselves on the deck. These women would look at her limping by and wonder why she was so happy.

The last day of the cruise, there was a talent show for all the tourists aboard the ship. My friend got up on stage to sing. But first she said, "You know, I want to say something to all of you ladies who have been watching me limp around the ship all week long. I know a lot of you are beautiful. You have wonderful figures. Your whole body is there . . . and obviously mine isn't. But I want you to understand something. I have learned through this trauma that *it's not how you walk* that matters in life, or whether you limp. What matters in life is *who you walk with*."

When she told me that story, I realized that here was a young lady who allowed God to tell her who she was. She understood that she was a child of *God*, and she realized that there were certain things she would do and things she wouldn't do.

Each of us has to ask whether or not we're letting God determine who we are.

If we do that, then we take the first step toward being able to push away peer pressure. If not, then we're being warped by the world.

So, the first thing to remember is who *you* are. But the second thing you need to keep in mind is who *they* are. "They" are whoever is putting the pressure on you to go against what you know to be God's will and what your conscience is telling you to do. Often when you're pressured to do something you know will violate your principles, you lose perspective. This person right there in your face seems so big and so important and so awesome.

It's as though you fear that if you say "no," that person's going to reject you, and your life will be destroyed. So, whenever you face that kind of test, you need to remember who these people are that you think are going to determine your future. The Bible says, "Don't worry so much about what other people think of you. That kind of mindset and lifestyle will ensnare you. Instead, be concerned about what *God* thinks of you. Trust in Him and you'll be kept safe" (Proverbs 29:25). In other words, if you live with fear of what this other person can do to you, you'll be trapped. It will ensnare you. It will keep hold of you. But if you just keep in mind who this other person is, you'll be freed from the pressure of doing what that person wants you to do. Your honor, fear, and respect will be going where it belongs—to God.

We must remember that God looks at humanity and sees that we are like grass in the field, which withers and dies. But He is infinite and eternal (Isaiah 40). We need to remember that the people who try to influence us are just a drop in the bucket—not because they lack importance, but because in comparison with God, their importance, even their collective strength, is nothing.

Now the point is that if I tell you I'm going to sic Pee Wee Herman on you, you won't be very intimidated. If I say I'm going to sic Hulk Hogan on you, you'll say, "Yes, I'll do whatever you want." Jesus said, "Do not be afraid of those who kill the body but can't kill the soul. Rather, be afraid of *God*, who can destroy both the body and the soul in hell" (Matthew 10:28). In other words, Jesus is telling us, "Get your perspective right."

If you want to be able to stand up against serious peer pressure, you're going to need to learn what it is to respect God and His view of who you are more than you respect what other people think about you. After all, what can this person do to you? You say, "Well, he could physically hurt me." Yeah, okay, he could hurt you. You say, "Well, he could also reject me." Yes, that's true also.

But the fact of the matter is that there

is a time when you need to choose conscience over cowardice. We need to choose what God wants us to do rather than just caving in to whatever anybody else out there wants.

So, you need to remember to let God tell you what you should be, and not let others tell you what to be. And there's just one more thing you've got to remember: *You need to keep eternity in your heart*. You see, when you're in the middle of this pressure, you have to remember that when you compare life here on earth against life in eternity, this little moment right now is not really so difficult and not really so long. We think, *Oh, no! I've got to cave in. There's just too much pressure.*

The irony is that just about everyone would be willing and able to stop caving in to the pressure to drink, cheat, steal, lie — whatever your weak spot may be — if someone offered you $1 million to resist this temptation for one week. So, what would keep you from doing it? Money! The real reason you would be able to keep from doing that sin is that you would be focusing more on the reward than you would on the pressure or the temptation. And when you focus more on the reward, the temptation or the pressure is not that big a deal.

In other words, if you have eternity in your heart, if God is telling you who you are, and if you remember who these other people are . . . what you begin to realize is that if you turn down this pressure or resist that temptation right now, you won't really have to hang on that much longer before you get your reward. You'll be able to hang tough right now because the reward of doing what's right is going to be (1) having no regret in your heart, (2) having a clear conscience, (3) having freedom before God, (4) knowing that you've done the right thing, and (5) experiencing the blessings and the benefits of obedience. So, what you need to do is focus on the reward and stand up to the peer pressure, because you're going to get a $1 million check from the Lord next week in the form of inner blessing and inner contentment.

The person who stands against the pressure has a different way of looking at things. If you have eternity in your heart, then you have a long-term perspective. You see that life in this world is kind of like a carnival, and sooner or later all of the lights are going to go off in the carnival, the power lines will be pulled, and all of the rides will stop. And then you'll have to go home.

A lot of people are caught up in the party. They're in the middle of doing whatever they want to do, riding the rides and watching the lights. These people don't realize that, hey, sooner or later, the carnival is going to shut down. Sooner or later it's going to be just you and your conscience standing before God. If you can remember that life is like a carnival—here today and gone tomorrow—it will be a lot easier for you to turn down the rides that are dangerous. In your heart you can say, "I'm not looking right now at just the thrill of this ride. I'm looking up the road."

For Reflection and Action

1. Describe a time when your friends persuaded you to do something that you knew was wrong. What did you learn from that experience?

2. Why do you think so many people choose to go against their conscience and do what they know is wrong just so they can be "cool" and not be "left out"? How important is it to you to be popular or cool?

3. Describe what a person acts like who chooses to honor God's opinion higher than people's opinions. What do you think God wants from you in your relationship with Him?

4. Consider your relationships with your friends. What kinds of changes do you need to make that would improve your decision-making in these relationships?

5. God wants you to live a life of personal freedom where you are not pressured by popular students at school or by your friends. True freedom means that you are free to let God, who knows what's best for your life, guide you into making the right decisions. Take some time this week to talk alone with God about how you want to make your own decisions and be your own person, not

letting pressure from your peers determine how you live.

For Meditation

The pressures to follow the crowd can really get to you—unless you make up your mind to step to the beat of a different drummer, as Thoreau said. Kick back and think about the following verse, because it has a lot to say to teens today.

> *Do not conform any longer to the pattern of this world, but be transformed by the renewing of your mind. Then you will be able to test and approve what God's will is—his good, pleasing and perfect will.* (Romans 12:2, *New International Version*)